TEMPORARY NOTEBOOK

TEMPORARY NOTEBOOK:

POEMS AND NON-HAIKU

SEB DOUBINSKY

STALKING HORSE PRESS - 10 YEARS
SANTA FE, NEW MEXICO

a rose is not a rose is not a rose
and will never be a rose

poetry isn't lists
lists are tools of power
lists are history-related
lists are excluding tools
lists are randomly biased
lists are cheap eroticism
lists are about listing things
lists are for people who do not get enough attention
lists are reactionary
shopping lists are lists
poems aren't lists

poetry isn't supposed
to make things
more complicated
poetry is supposed
to destroy things

what will happen
when capitalism is gone?
what will fill the void
and who will wear the party hats?
who will break the drums
and set the garlands on fire?
who will put coins in the jukebox
and who will dance with the empty dress?

night hangs outside
like a homeless on the corner
hoodie down on its eyes
waiting for nothing
and having nowhere to go

the tic tic of the mind
the crack crack of the bones
the boom boom of the heart
so low so low so low
and yet deafening

the huge cold night
the splendidly useless stars
the eyes powerless and watching
the eyes containing more light than the day

you wonder if you exist
but does the leaf that falls
wonder if the tree exists?

I never wonder

I accept
and admire
both the leaf
the tree
and the turning
of the season

things we show
are seldom seen
as the eye
only selects
the visible

is poetry fiction
with a visible structure
or reality
without a visible structure?

thinking about Paris
I realize
that my youth
lies in the morgue there
waiting for someone
to identify it
from its tattoos, bruises
and lipstick traces

this poem never goes to church
this poem never prays
this poem watches the wind in the trees
and listens to the song of invisible birds
this poem thinks churches make beautiful ruins
where more trees can grow and more birds can sing

(On the Notre-Dame fire, April 2019)

I wanted to give you something
not anything
something unique yes
but I didn't find anything
so here is a little nothing
that isn't something
and could be anything
but is unique
nonetheless

(For Sofie, on her birthday.)

five little birds on a branch
a hand of feathers and songs

The way we treat our dead:
we close the book
and gently kiss the cover
before we put it back
in our favorite shelf

the sun opens the curtains
the birds sing me a good morning song
I feel like a king without a kingdom
a king free of power and violence
a king free to enjoy the day
with or without a paper crown

I am here
you can see me
I am not waiting for anything
but I am here nonetheless
neither friend nor foe
but here
for you
just so you know
you do exist
and you can breathe
you can breathe all you want
it's alright
because I am here
to witness your undeniable existence
I am here
and all fear me
except you

heavy clouds roll over the garden
the wind messes the flowers' hair
the smell of the afternoon coffee stays still
— imaginary movement of the nostrils

this poem is a late poem
there could be a moon
there could be clouds
there could be stars even
but no
only the hour and the shadow
and the creepy sleep
and the empty dreams
and the deep pillow
to hug as a dead friend

there is
in the middle of the body
an emptiness
that makes the heart
resound like a music instrument

quiet quiet quiet
is the night inside the room
only disturbed once in a while
by the quick flash of a dream
and the halted breath of the sleeper

the failure of poetry
is its triumph
ruins more beautiful
than steel and concrete

the night squeezes
through the half open window
quietly quietly quietly
like an expected lover
who tries to surprise you
but fails beautifully

my feet under the sheets
have a life of their own
creating mountains and valleys
and crazy frozen landscapes
while I am trying to focus on my life
— oh how I envy
the freedom they have
these little feet of mine!

when you have no idea
what to write about
then not-writing becomes the idea
and the world can at last unfold itself
in your non-imaginary glass of wine

counting the pearls
in my hand
I find three
one for you
one for you
and another one for you
which I give you to keep
but my hand is not empty now
it is filled with the memory of these gifts

rain and wind in the garden
two birds dart by and land in a tree
I watch them from my window
like a ghost watches the living
from the comfort of its death

who are we
when the name has been given
and forgotten?
a hand holding an empty glass
a memory yet to unfold
or a shadow longing for light?
who are we
when the name has been erased by mistake?
when the name has been crushed by a rock?
when the name has been deformed and
transformed?
a laughter suppressed in the throat
a panic larger than your own home
or an absolute freedom
unlimited by hearts, bricks and concrete?

This poem will not rhyme
this poem is on strike
this poem will not be intimidated
in any way
this poem will not rhyme
until justice is achieved for all
this poem will not rhyme
until women are paid like men
this poem will not rhyme
until all can benefit from retirement
this poem will not rhyme
until the rich pay their taxes
this poem will not rhyme
— for equality
for justice
for respect for all
this poem will not rhyme

"I am nothing"
you sometimes say
forgetting that it takes
a body, many dreams, some nightmares,
a home, a city, a region, a land,
a sun, a moon, an infinity of stars
a whole planet, an entire galaxy
for you to utter those words

the leaves rustle
in the warm afternoon
— reading

is emptiness full of emptiness?
is noise full of silence
and silence of noise?

a bird lands on a branch
so high
I can barely see it

a temporary touch of color
among the familiar leaves

poetry isn't words

clouds glide like silver knives
on the throat of the sky

we stare in awe at our new car
a banknote flutters by like an expensive butterfly

we will never know the depth of our ignorance

poetry inserted like wisdom teeth
in our badly shattered jaws

somewhere an old president dies

in the garden the cat moves like a tiny panther
two birds fly away

gray sky no clouds

I drink my coffee without thinking

only the bitterness remains
followed by the comfort of sugar

the gas station disappears
behind us in the night
like a Chinese lantern
drifting on a dark ocean

you wave goodbye
I wave goodbye
the waves wave
the waves always wave

the wind bends
the grassy dunes' copper spears
— peace in violence

big golden coin
to buy nothing
the moon is mine tonight

this empty chair
is my throne
it creaks when I sit down

what are the divinities
but invisible friends
playful and kind?

some poets write on marble
others paint or compose symphonies
— I sketch

rain in August
and suddenly
the melancholy of autumn
taps on the window

the sun rises
between the careful hands
of the sky
like a blinding child

life lies in the grass
not on the path

muses hate poets
they think they are creeps
and hate to be objectified
so, poets,
if you see a muse in a bar
leave her alone
and write about something else
like your shitty love life

heatwave
— everything moves
in slow motion
and slightly tastes of salt

sometimes beauty is just
a butterfly set aflame by the sun
burning nothing
but bringing light
to the flowers and the trees

"this way" she said
meaning "that way"
— the story of poetry

we are the only species
trying to turn the sun, the sea.
the forests, animals
and even ourselves
into gold
— we are the alchemists of Death

a dead bird in the garden
the others keep singing
only the branch seems to miss it

when your eyelids turn to marble
you know that statues do dream

autumn sits at my garden table
an elegant lady in gray
slightly teary and smelling of the last roses

we walk under the gray clouds
thinking about an invisible menace
while a few birds sing
invisible too

two lines about the weather
are more than enough
and yet

we are all fools
running along the path
laughing at other fools
who are laughing at us
when we should be
sitting side by side by the road
enjoying the warmth of the rising sun
and listening to the trickster stories
of the playful wind

rain slaps my face
like a violent pearl-curtain
the world is a huge wet house
built outside in

night weighs almost nothing
but day is like bars of gold in a suitcase
— you have to leave it behind if you want to
survive

today I celebrate all those
forgotten by celebrations
I celebrate those in the shadow
those in the cracks those in the gaps
I celebrate the uneasy and the shy
the lame and the weak
I celebrate the reprobate and the sneaky
the sullen and the mute
today I celebrate the uncelebrated
today I celebrate you

the moon shines and gives us new shadows
whereas the sun gives our shadows new bodies
we pass through silence and noise
never ourselves but always the same

we are so tiny tiny
and the world is so huge so huge
only our heart can measure up
and turn us into giants

when you look out of your window
you do not see any direction
yet you enjoy the view
why should life be any different?

the eyes close
the limbs weaken
sleep sips in through
the half-open lips
and breath is reversed
-- the world becomes dreams
and we, the immortal travelers

the defeat of words
is not the death of language
nor the ultimate illumination
— it is the song of the river over the rocks
or the laughter of the clouds
pushed by the moon

the Tao of failure
is the most difficult to master
but also the only one
that encompasses everything

the silence in us is not death
it is not life either
it is us, in between,
as we truly are

the purpose of water is water
the purpose of fire is fire
the purpose of wind is wind
the purpose of life is life
and that's it

a pale sun is still the sun
dusk is still the day
nuances are what separate
melancholy from despair

poetry is poetry
life is life
poetry isn't life
life isn't poetry
yet one cannot exist
without the other
— oh the beautiful frailty
of man-made things!

this poem
bathed in the mainstream
and is still rubbing its skin
to get the fucking tar off

waking up
is easier
than staying awake
— ask the late blooming rose
gently swaying in the autumn breeze

poetry can move mountains
and if it can move mountains
it can move you
it is very strong
way stronger than you think

my body is like a drying leaf
as autumn moves in
— not changing colors
but feeling the sap
get heavier and scarcer
and the weight of my memories
becoming lighter and lighter
waiting for the first breeze
to blow them away
so they can land
in someone else's garden
and be crushed
under a laughing child's feet

life is
a temporary
notebook

the quiet hum of the street
half a sun and a cup of coffee
I stretch —— my bones crack
making my skull grin under my aging skin
the bird in the tree takes off in a blur

the day changes
clouds gather for tea
birds eat the crumbs
everybody is looking forward
for the night
and the strange guests it brings

the sun paints
a moon
on my face

I am the eclipse

you don't write poetry
to be read
you write poetry
so you can breathe

salt scattered
on the dark tablecloth
stars in the sky
— as above so below

a bird flies by my window
in a diagonal of feathers

poetry lies outside language

Seb Doubinsky is a bilingual writer born in Paris in 1963. His novels and poetry collections have been published in France, the UK and in the USA. He currently lives with his family in Aarhus, Denmark, where he teaches at the university.